BROKEN Silence

James R. Dixon

iUniverse, Inc.
Bloomington

Broken Silence

iUniverse books may be ordered through booksellers or by contacting:

iUniverse
1663 Liberty Drive
Bloomington, IN 47403
www.iuniverse.com
1-800-Authors (1-800-288-4677)

ISBN: 978-1-4620-7256-9 (sc)
ISBN: 978-1-4620-7257-6 (e)

Library of Congress Control Number: 2011962316

Printed in the United States of America

iUniverse rev. date: 12/13/2011

I like to say the quiet ones have the most to say, but it's getting others to hear them that's the problem. After The Other Me I think a few people finally hear me to say the least. With that said, Broken Silence is the breakthrough from an individual being a prisoner of his or herself. Have you ever had so much to say, but no one to say it to? Have you ever felt like you constantly had to explain yourself to others who find you too different to be acceptable? Broken Silence is my outlet to explain myself for the benefit of others to understand me. For years I've been prosecuted by others who don't approve of me being myself, or me openly discussing some of my trials and tribulations. For some reason it seems that I encounter a lot of people who pretend to live in this perfect world where problems don't exist. I'm definitely not ashamed to admit the fact that I don't.

I express my feelings about my heartache in the relationship department and personal situations. I also provide solutions to enhance society. Those who have placed stereotypes upon me due to the color of my skin along with those who've underestimated me are my biggest inspiration for the formation of this poetry book. Searching for peace to unwind, this book provided me the opportunity to release built up tension. Broken Silence is the extension of The Other Me (My Moment of Honesty) in the sense that it's broken into the same four sections. The poems in my love side, emotional side, resilient side, and good side serve as the breakthrough from the mischievous emotions once clouding my mind.

What I hope to accomplish with this book is to give inspiration to those who find it hard to digest the hurtful words of misjudgment by others who aren't secure with themselves. The message I would like others to receive is to be confident and strong. Understand that just because we all have problems doesn't mean we have to be victims of what we've done. Find a mature outlet to deal with your problems and make future situations better.

The Love Side of Broken Silence is based on a severely broken relationship. Once being in love, you feel things are so blissful to the point it's difficult to imagine an epic fail. Imagine doing everything so perfect for someone to the point it changes your outlook on life. Things like building someone's confidence, helping to raise someone's self esteem, and loving someone with everything you have. Sounds great right? But due to that person's insecurities, the relationship goes through a downward spiral. Because you don't flinch about any of it, suddenly all negative events that took place become your fault. After the break up, your former partner blames you for all negative actions that has occurred in her past that you had no control over and weren't even around for. All of the constant arguing and emotional heartache changes the positive outlook you once had that seemed to be blissful.

In the Emotional Side of Broken Silence, I poetically discuss some of my trials and tribulations. A few trials that I shed light on revolve around issues that exist in my life today. Some tribulations I explain are reminiscent to my past. In addition to that, I also discuss horrendous truths about the misfortunes of other people that I've witnessed.

The Resilient Side of Broken Silence gets pretty hot and heavy. I share a lot of situations that I had to overcome to be the person I consider myself to be today. A lot of situations discussed in this section are extremely controversial. I talk about my experiences with racism, insolence of despicable people, and personal triumph just to name a few.

Through the controversy with personal issues, emotional situations, and relationship heartache, we send Broken Silence off on a good note. The Good Side of Broken Silence provided the space for me to focus on the benevolence of my actions. Everything from charity, trendsetting, and self confidence are displayed in this portion of the book. Hopefully this section sheds light on a few things we need to do in our lives to elevate the prosperity in society.

Contents

Love Side

Fool Of Me

When I look into your eyes
  It's hard for me to believe
    You don't recognize the signs
     I like you and want you to adore me
      My sunshine
       Turn my fantasy into reality
      As you unwind
        Visualize a future with me
          Or at least this was what I wanted for us
         I'm unclear if you wanted this from me
           Though this whole time I'm begging love
           To stop making a fool of me

When I look at my life
  I don't see you with me
   I feel lonely inside
    In need of your company indeed
     My sunshine
      Is occupied though I wish was reserved for me
       So I explain to you that I visualize
        You and me in emotional harmony
         Or at least this was what I wanted for us
        I'm unclear if you wanted this from me
         Though this whole time I'm begging love
         To stop making a fool of me

Tainted Love

Recognize
          Fantasize
                    Visualize

Me thinking of you while you think of me
Our thoughts emotionally entwining
While our hearts harmonize
Singing a song deeper than Mary J Blige
Deep penetration inside you to relax after a long day
Champagne on the night stand to take the stress away
Then I heard something I didn't want to believe
Me and another man shared your same intimacy
Your response was "can't we all be free"
The love sounds good to you, but it sounds tainted to me

Recognize
          Fantasize
                    Visualize

Our love experienced on a new plateau
And getting higher; your elevated feelings for me is what I desire
It burns me like fire; when it comes down to the wire
I will do anything to appease you
It comforts me to satisfy and please you
I love you! Please believe my feelings are true
Then I heard something I didn't want to believe
You gave another man the same speech you gave me
Your response was "he like you showed interest in me"
The love sounds good to you, but it sounds tainted to me

Love Is Blind

Till death do us part
That was the commitment I wanted from you
I've invested everything
Even defended you against my own family
Without you my heart suffered
A long summer blight
Followed by a cold winter
Full of many sleepless nights
I would cry in my sleep
Wishing you were there
To replenish a broken heart
Currently in despair
Those in my past polluted my air
But you were a fresh breathe
I'd always panic for my phone
To check for a missed call or a text
The sound of your voice
Helped to relieve my distress
Along with the quiet nights
When I'd rest my head on your chest

Marriage was soon to follow
As this sounded like the perfect picture
Then reality instantly sets it
It was revealed you were only with me to get richer
But look at the big picture
I asked you to be the mother of my kids
When one minute you hated my guts
Then the next you could care less if I lived
Threatening my livelihood
By posting embarrassing pictures of things I did
Threatening to discard birth control pills to sabotage our relationship
Forcing our potential infants to become bastards
By not allowing their father to see his children
The moment I got my publishing deal, you were the first to witness
Assuming we were going to live in sin
In the piece of real estate I purchased
I'm unaware if you've heard this
But I don't condone
You using me as your stepping stone
To get ahead, but you're still worthless

Senryu Intermission

Love is blind and has
Impaired my vision
In time it will heal for me

Love is blind! The second you let your guard down too far it will take over your mind.

Frustration Within A Nation

Our styles were different
    Mine was inspirational
        Whereas you wanted someone

Who would let you do what you wanted to do
    Screw who you wanted to screw
        But I wouldn't let you

Do what you wanted to do
    As I felt my way was the best way
        And your way others couldn't relate

They couldn't help but to debate
    The idiotic methods of your transformation
        Which led to undesirable emancipation

Bringing about broken spirits
    And shattered dreams
        No self respect, low self-esteem

No sense of self worth
    As it's been thrown in back of a hearse
        Meant to be buried beneath my feet

Oh so depressing
    And extremely frustrating
        It was to think of you with me

The Great Annoyance

Since the day we split my frustration has erected
Due to my heart being neglected
I was truly disrespected
Rest assured you folded under the pressure
Your insecurities were the worst
As you would play the victim role
When you weren't even hurt
You solely got on my nerves
Arguing with me every chance you had
You wondered why I always got mad
I was tired of you crying when you were sad
And trying to gain sympathy to make me feel bad
Especially when you brought this all on yourself
After all, it was you who threw me on the shelf
I was obviously not what you wanted
Now you're calling me claiming your nights are haunted
By the ghost of me in which you fear to see
But you won't get a tear from me
So I then got the impression you tried to trap me
By claiming you were pregnant and I was the daddy

But the reality is your attitude is jacked up
Yelling like a fire breathing dragon so I backed up
You only made yourself look stupid
As I learned to ignore you and got used to it
I felt like I was walking on egg shells around you
Watching every word I said so you wouldn't claim I hurt you
With everyone else, your mouth was so steek
For someone with a loud bark, your bite was so weak
But when it came to me, you were fierce when confronting me
Yelling, **Fussing**, **Screaming**, and **Cussing**
Finally I found joy in that being all over
And you wanted it to start again, but it was over

Ungrateful

Just when the doubts were out that you would never make it
The show stopper stepped in, picked up the show, and saved it
Before me you were a drunken slob, fully intoxicated
I revamped your lifestyle, but did you ever appreciate it?
I took you from ghetto to class and props you started to take it
I stripped your hands of the alcohol so your life wouldn't get wasted
Your girlfriends were jealous! Seeing us together, they began to hate it
I made you popular, but did you ever appreciate it?

Degrading your body by wearing low cut tops to show your D-Cups
You went from dressing slutty to a classy senorita
Due to my improvements on you everyone was desperate to meet us
I gave you your self-respect, but did you ever appreciate it?
I put you in school and finally got you out of the clubs
I introduced you to classy men rather than dating thugs
Before me you made it rain; because of me you now make it flood
I provided you with diamonds instead of studs, but did you ever appreciate it?

I got you to believe the day you met me was pure fate

I got you off the cheeseburgers and now you're losing weight

At first you couldn't buy a man, but now you have dates

Your life was depressing until I made it great, but did you ever appreciate it?

I got you thinking positive by pulling you out of that evil mind state

With your new attitude people won't be tempted to slap you in your face

You were once gay until I converted you straight

I gave you a new life, but did you ever appreciate it?

All I ever wanted was a thank you! You're so ungrateful!

Cold December

Brace yourself for a Cold December
Tell me if you remember

Brace yourself for a Cold December

As you will be spending it alone this winter

You pushed me out of your life; I hope you remembered

The times we had and things I've done since September

Of the year before as it won't happen anymore

Your childish antics and temper tantrums

Should be non-existent; you're twenty-eight

It's sad you still live life this way

Brace yourself for a Cold December
Tell me if you remember

Tell me if you remember

Your jealous ways and underhanded display

Of a mature woman; it was all just a cover

Like your positive attitude and words you spoke to my mother

As they were all lies which meant you put up a front

Like an Oscar nominated actress telling all the lies you want

As time passed I began to see right through you

You're a boozer! You're not confident and strong! You're a loser!

Brace yourself for a Cold December!

Senryu Intermission

I once felt lucky
To have you
Now I feel lucky
To have you gone

I poured my heart and soul to you only to get ignored. Then you taunted me for lacking emotional forbearance. You annoyed me with your constant blaming, crying, and complaining. You annoyed me by humming the tune of your same old song.

Virgin

When the sun fades, rain shall restore

As my love for you exist no more

I used to spend my nights thinking about how we fought

You were the forefront of my mind, now you're an after thought

Soon to be forgotten due to your lack of gratitude

The bitter judgments you pass provoke your attitude

The hell I've experienced wasn't worth the price of keeping you

As the calamitous words you spoke became true

You met your match with me and weren't ready for this

All the while I waited for you to admit, you weren't ready to commit

You lost your composure and strength; you became an emotional wreck

You don't have the mental capabilities to handle a relationship

I wouldn't dare ask you to come back because I wanted you to leave

To make my life worth living and become stress free

You brought pain to me and ignorance; you see

I'm better off without you and my conscience is free

Brokenhearted

You are **coldhearted**; I am **brokenhearted**
You physically corrupted me; I emotionally trusted you
You are **ruthless** and **condescending**
I was foolish to believe

That you and me would last for eternity

I am **brokenhearted** that you're so **coldhearted**
I fully loved you; you took advantage of me
You are **selfish** and **disrespecting**
I was foolish to believe

That you and me would last for eternity

Resentment is all over my face from not letting you go away
The first time you chose to leave I shouldn't have retrieved

Now you're withdrawn for good and I can finally be free
From your **ruthless**, **condescending**, **selfish**, and **disrespecting** deeds

Senryu Intermission

Patience is a virtue
In which you didn't
Possess any with me

Your insane actions that were caused by inebriation are the reasons you need anger management. I'm curious to know how you can look yourself in the mirror without vomiting.

Misery Loves Company

Third time is said to be a charm, but turned out that it wasn't
So what do I make of dating you as I felt my time was a waste

Good times were minimal, but then it becomes clear
You were brought here to teach me a lesson
About karma as they say what goes around comes around
I've been around with you on more than one occasion

There was no coronation
I would constantly hit the ground
Many said I would rue the day that I met you
The thought of it made me cry as I would deny
Somehow I was in love and was morally blind
My feelings for you left faster than they came in my sights
From being disgusted in your behavior
Despicable you who bowed to alcohol as your savior

Only to become a raging drunk
More than what you already was
It should've been nothing more than lust
How the hell did I fall in love?

Maybe I was drunk, or hurting in my heart
So you capitalized at the expense of my vulnerability
But rather than continue
You get a thank you from me
Because being around you
Helped me realize what I don't want to be

Pathetic, weak, a loser, and a dead beat!
You're dead to me; you no longer exist!

Hypnotized Mind

Every time I spoke to you

                                         You sounded like you were in a trance

You never got the reaction you wanted

                                         Simultaneously you ignored my advance

So now I understand; I get it

                                         I'm a visionary; you're a witness

I'm a witness to your lack of vision

                                         Prosperity for you died and has no longer risen

That explains why you wanted me back

                                         Questioning my involvement with another woman

Raising hell in my face; causing drama behind my back

                                         Giving me flack about every woman I contact

Then everything you bought you asked for it back

                                         I'm on an emotional rollercoaster

I'm dying to get off

                                         Make up your mind because you're running out of time

One minute you say you love me

                              The next you want me out of your life

Constantly screaming and cussing

                        Making yourself out to be the victim in every fight

I consider you dead weight

                          There's no way I can prosper with you around

Just when I thought I was ahead you'd stack the deck

                    Consider psychiatric help; you're an emotional wreck

Because you're lonely
You want others to be
Miserable like you

Alcohol abuse and a ten word vocabulary pretty much define your personality. You're twenty-eight years old with no education, or career goals desperate to find a man to provide you with a place to call home.

Wonder Woman

All is fair in love and war
But this isn't war
This is love versus
You trying to settle a score
You stopped giving me the time of day
So I tried to forget about you
How difficult you made that for me
Your body is off the hinges
Nowhere near the brink of extinction
I can't get exhausted with you
You keep my heart wrenching
In pain from not having what it took
To get your attention
Once I compared the moment I thought of you
To the moment I first saw you
I began to realize
How much I wanted you back in my life

Then quickly in strife

You took control of my emotions in stride

I then could relate to you

As I began to meditate

You began to alleviate

The pain bestowed upon me

From the day that I first met you

You will soon regret the day I let you

Walk away for good because there will be no return

Broken Promises

I can't believe I was too blind to see you were leading me on
I felt like an idiot; more or less I felt played
I expressed my love for you
Just to find out you never felt the same way
I wonder if your husband would've condoned us going on a date
And you introducing your child to me as if I was your soul mate
I prayed things would be different; yet again I made the same mistake
Of trusting treacherous women whose intentions are fake

Calling my phone every late night claiming God has cursed me
My husband keeps cheating on me and would constantly hurt me
I was ready to declare you number one on my roster
Whereas with your husband you were on his reserve
He uses you for sexual implications and makes you feel like an imposter
As for me, I vowed to give you everything you deserved
As I sit and reminisce on the conversations we had; I came to the conclusion
They meant more to me than they did to you in the past

You made me feel on top of the world where no one can stop me
That fall night my vision was me under you as you were on top of me
That winter should've been the birth of my child; I wonder who was blocking me
I was enraged fist to cuffs while you were begging me to stop and freeze
Demonic? Please! You never seen me express feelings this diabolically
With numerous anxiety attacks, I needed psychiatric care to sponsor me
And for God to follow me, talk to me, walk with me
Alleviate this pain from these visions that are haunting me

I wanted so bad to build a home for you to live
I'm not saying it's your fault, but without you look what I did
I dated an alcoholic whose ill-tempered fire was lit
Who mistreated me; I caught the backlash from every man in her past she let hit
My next encounter was with a woman who downplayed God, marriage, and children
Who spent more money on alcohol then she did on her rent
She woke up hung over every morning questioning where her last night was spent
Drunk dialing me in mid-afternoon to hear her heart vent

The next woman I fell in love with I thought was the one
I was blinded by luxurious things I didn't see her attitude up front
She was argumentative! She would only express her feelings when she was drunk
Light switch was off in her head as she would sing before the bell rung
That was strike three! I officially struck out at bat
Emotionally unstable I was as I dealt you the facts
I was hurt, broken, crushed, and emotionally flat
Can you envision my pain and heartache? You could've saved me from all of that!

Emotional Side

Pain Is Love

The Eyes Never Lie

I Miss You

No Security

Love With The Lights On

Self Destruct

Broken Woman

Good Girls Like Bad Guys

Changes

The Moon And The Stars

Another Place

Get Away

Pain Is Love

Pain is love
But at what point does love have to become pain
Love should be sustained
A destiny ordained
But I felt physical and emotional pain
As you were striking me in vain
Your weapons piercing my skin and veins
Causing my bones to catapult into my brain
Internal bleeding, I never felt something so strange
And it was me that you blamed
Bringing this upon myself is what you had claimed
You walk around proclaiming
You're this great person, but you're insane
I begged and pleaded for you to stop
But you were mentally deranged

Pain is love
But that wasn't love
That was destruction caused by an ill-tempered maniac
To an adolescent essence
I was supposed to be a testament
An extension of you
Now I have the same tension as you
But I release it differently

The Eyes Never Lie

There I sat in the cold stormy weather alone
Feeling torn and partially disowned
Each raindrop that rolled down my window
Was a replica of the tears rolling down the windows of my soul

He pushed me out of the way as he proceeded to leave
He walked out so fast I questioned if he cared for me
With no financial, or emotional support he became a dead beat
I was always known as his son although he wasn't a father to me

Stand up and be a man, but that was too much to ask from
A man who professionally cowardly runs
Away from his responsibilities and debts he owed to my sister
Low life scum he is and we all saw this as the big picture

I used to cry for you, but at one point all the tears stopped
Instantly when I realized you're so cold hearted you never let a tear drop
It shows how much you don't care so maybe I should care less
But the windows of my soul are open to suppress

Senryu Intermission

How can one person
Make you feel so small
And continue to sleep well

It was hard for me to believe you were so determined to dismantle my humanity. Very soon you will understand it was your humanity that you initially dismantled. Due to your actions, your true colors were put on display.

I Miss You

As my poetic journey continues I want to take a step back
To remember a loved one who passed
Grandma, I really miss you to the point I can't sleep
I can't breathe and when I think about you I get weak

Your flesh is destroyed but your spirit lives in me
It flourishes and comforts me when I feel weak
It didn't hit me you passed away until months later
When I stopped by your house to take you to Staters

To take you grocery shopping and no one was aware
That I pulled half way in your drive way to realize you weren't there
As I broke down I remembered all of the good times
And things you've done for me in your time

With all the sweets you made, your house was like a bakery
As we would eat and enjoy your stories about slavery
Singing songs that followed the stories you told
About Harriet Tubman inspired by the underground railroad

You were a beautiful woman, but your strength was your best feature
Although I never took you for a reader
You read me stories about Martin, Malcolm, and Farrakhan
To inspire me to be a great person and teach me how to be a leader

It was hard to accept the fact your house was no longer in our family
It was home away from home because your neighbors could stand me
Living around the way from you made your time worth stealing
Going to your house always felt like a family reunion

I moved far away from you, but I still fell in line
I used to be greedy by demanding all of your time
I didn't want to share you; time with you I was craving
I loved you so much my girlfriends back then would hate me

Even though my siblings didn't pick up on your message
It's been instilled in me so I am living proof
Of the example you set and what you've said all along
I'm going to be successful before it's all said and done

What I wouldn't do to give you one more hug
Sometimes I hug myself to envision me showing you love
I can't wait till the day I see you again
But until then, I recap the memories we shared back then

My fondest memories of you were when I was seven
I love you, I miss you, and I know you're watching me from heaven
These aren't my final words, but just my current thoughts
For more time with you I definitely should've fought

No Security

You've provided no security
The relationship was full of unjust treatment
Your parsimonious ways should've been abolished
If you treated her anything like you treated your Cadillac
She'd be smooth and polished
Rather than being shined
She's wounded
Her skin scarred by the rubbing of sand paper
Similar to the words you speak
Made her heart weak
Your childish antics are shameful
Playing games as if you were in preschool
You tearing her down
To build yourself up was only the prequel
To your sequel

You've provided no security
The relationship was full of unjust treatment
When your life was a three ring circus
She was the lion who tamed it
And this is how you repay her
Through the abandonment of her children
Total lack of respect
What did you really have to offer
Besides a bulk of lies
That can fit inside the tomb of Khafre

You've provided no security
The relationship was full of unjust treatment
How dare you treat her this way
She gave up her whole life to make you happy
And you made her cry
Why?
Was it the fact you acted like a little kid
Throwing temper tantrums at random
Why?
Was it that you couldn't take no for an answer
Yelling and cussing
Acting like you're God's gift to the planet
Sorry to break it to you but you're not
Your life is a flop

Senryu Intermission

Life is too short
Be appreciative of what you have
In your life

You only live once. Don't live your life wondering what if. You forfeit half of the benefits from the opportunities you don't take.

Love With The Lights On

Irresponsible teenage girls is nothing new to me
So how do you explain them having babies
Before they complete puberty
As the lights go off they open their legs fluently

Low self-esteem-No direction
Low self respect-No reflection

Blessings were soon to come to you as you felt daunted
A young boy sweet talks you and makes you feel wanted
He claims to love you to have sex with you; his intentions are wrong
Encouraging you to have unprotected sex as he pulls down your thong
Singing you a song as you're diagnosed with pregnancy
He up and leaves; he's not ready to be a father
You considering aborting your baby is man slaughter
Then nine months later you pop up with a daughter

High pain-Much stress
Highly insane-Much distress

Now you're in the same position as your mother
How do you like it?
Being the mother of an irresponsible daughter
How will you fight it?
Maybe now you'll be more appreciative of your mother
As you go crying back to her, your sisters, and your brother

The shameful part is there is no common sense inside your dome
   You party with your friends leaving your starving baby at home
      Your priorities are wrong so failure must be an option
         In order for you to elect to put your child up for adoption

         Putting what little ounce of integrity you have in jeopardy
      All five percent of it; the other ninety-five percent is the recipe
   Of what you need to be a real woman and handle your responsibility
But your brain is filled with stupidity and idiocy

It seems you're only good for flooding your face with makeup
   Isolating your real friends for the fake ones and acting stuck up
      As life moves fast you try to move faster
         By thinking you're grown and your parent's opinions don't matter

         The truth is you should listen because you're not so smart
      If you were then you wouldn't have loved in the dark
   Love with the lights on and be appreciative of what you have
A gift you don't share with just anyone who's up for grabs

Self Destruct

She couldn't stand the position she was in
It was making her throttle
As she began to expand her search for a new life
At the bottom of a vodka bottle

Her enraged boyfriend would strike her every other night
Then beg her to stay, but to her dismay she stayed
Due to her being too afraid to leave; she couldn't stand him
She blamed society for her self respect getting broke and decrepit

She's very argumentative and her words are relentless
Like daggers to your heart as she makes it pretentious
She envisions being attacked which then makes you look suspicious
So she attacks you coercing you to be a witness
To the self destruction of a woman once truly gifted
Settle down is what you tell her as that only makes her more vicious
Anger turns into rage and as mentioned
She's very argumentative and her words are relentless

Broken Woman

How can I sleep with so much pain to a life
As I came across a young girl laying in fright
She laid defenseless bleeding from her head to her waistline
As I panicked to get her medical treatment before she died
A young promiscuous girl dying to change her life
She refused to give up her goods
So a man struck her that night
Now trust only goes so far
For other men in her life
Because she makes countless trips
To her local doctor's spot
To receive hepatitis shots
To determine if she's caught an STD or not
Her lifeline is in danger as she fears she won't make it
For a month revenge was the hottest topic on twitter
A man threatening to do bodily harm
To the man who nearly murdered his sister
Then later claimed it was a publicity stunt to get richer
But this young girl is the big picture
She can't seem to trust anyone
It seems her family abandoned her
A year after the birth of her son
That marked the turning point of her life as a dancer
Meanwhile her struggle included the diagnosis of cancer

As if all of this hardship wasn't enough
There's a little more to the story of a girl who had it rough
Little did I know that young girl was a grown woman
Who had a bounty over her head
Guys willing to rape her for money
The sad part is her friends obviously thought it was funny
As they left her alone with a sexual predator
Who wouldn't allow her to go home
Instead he raped her and split her dome
Stripped her of her livelihood and everything she owned
He should be locked away and stoned
Vigorously by those he physically harmed alone
He was then found on the site of another demoralizing sexcapade
His soul diminished like the woman's spirit
It took a while but the woman was cured and the best fact
Is that she beat cancer, overcame adversity, and got her life back

Good Girls Like Bad Guys

WHEN GOOD GIRLS

Who are career oriented, beautiful, and well educated
Seemingly has the world in her hands becomes elated
Lays down a life plan that most of her peers hated
They wouldn't sacrifice it for anyone or demand it be traded

LIKES BAD GUYS

Who are unstable, dead beats, and uneducated
Seemingly has nothing to live for and no reason to be elated
Mooches off their parents with no life plans and are hated
Try to bring others down and wish their lives were traded

THE RESULT IS

They physically fight due to the feeling of being underappreciated
Multiple surgeries occur due to you being physically castrated
You deny him sex so he rapes you only to make you a statistic updated
Or the worst case scenario, your home becomes crime scene investigated

I DON'T UNDERSTAND

Why a woman dumps a man
Because they feel he's too nice
Only to date a loser
Who demands control over her life
He beats her then takes advantage
For the life of me I don't understand it
After two black eyes, a busted lip, and a broken arm
You stay with him although you're damaged
Your excuse is "it's because I love him"
So you defend him against those who judge him
He lies repeatedly, but you continue to trust him
All in all your excuse is still "because I love him"
He destroyed the home you happily built
He gets you pregnant and leaves because he has no life skills

LADIES
If this is your definition of love
You should change it before it gets you killed

Senryu Intermission

The soul of this woman
Has crumbled
By his abuse!
Was she to blame?

Allowing someone to impose their will on you can leave you lifeless. Not recovering from the imposition can leave you breathless.

Changes

The landscape of the game,

Has officially been changed!

Sometimes I ask myself,

Where do I fit in?

Do I even fit in at all?

Is there a place for me?

Or should I build a wall?

To block out those who block me!

It's obvious they don't want me,

To be part of the family!

So they isolate themselves to exclude me

When I wanted so bad to be included

      It's crazy how this once was my world

      Now I feel like I'm losing

My friends and I parted ways

My family doesn't find me amusing

      A former acquaintance became bland

      She downplayed marriage and children

But what I found amusing

Was the fact that she got pregnant by an abusive man

      I just don't understand

      Why people make bad changes

But change can be good for me in time!

Change is a growing process and a part of my life!

The Moon And The Stars

I wish life was sweet like the moon and the stars!
Where we could sleep in the light and avoid the dark!

When many of you were wishing for luxurious things
I was wishing my father would support my dreams
Support me rather than control everything
Feed me to prevent enduring pain and suffering
Talk to me; walk with me so I wouldn't feel alone
Teach me life lessons I could use when I'm grown
Teach me to respect women rather than treat them like property I own
Be an Indian and allow me to be grown

I wish life was sweet like the moon and the stars!
Where we could sleep in the light and avoid the dark!

When many of you were wishing for amazing friends
I was wishing the days of my backstabbing friends would come to an end
Stop impregnating girls who are barely over the age of ten
Refrain from being defeated by life and worry about where your time is spent
Stop making illegal money to pay two percent of your mother's rent
Get a real job to financially support your children
After making bad decisions don't call me to come to your defense
Don't play up to me in person when you don't consider me a friend

I wish life was sweet like the moon and the stars!
Where we could sleep in the light and avoid the dark!

When many of you were wishing for a world with bright sense
I was wishing I lived in a better environment
Where people wouldn't blame others for their own detriment
And I could focus more on creating an early retirement
People would be enthused to lead and not go where the followers went
Instead of being envious of hard workers, give a compliment
Help the less fortunate rather than intoxicate your body with poison
Build yourself up and understand you can't help the poor if you're one of them

I wish life was sweet like the moon and the stars!
Where we could sleep in the light and avoid the dark!

Life is what you make it
I am determined
To make the best of mine

As I make myself more adaptable to change I acquiesce myself wholeheartedly in a business plan to accomplish my life goals.

Another Place

I'm verbally volatile how should I be

When I'm irritated my attitude gets the best of me

I feel I always lose and can't win with you next to me

I need you gone in order for me to be stress free

With you here I do things I can't believe

I'm emotionally taunting and physically haunting

My verbal insulting needs to be clean

Spiraling out of control isn't my destiny

You were supposed to be a good influence on me

But you made my life bad instantly

You brought me back to a place I never wanted to be

Now how do I pack my bags to retreat

I want to be in another place

A place where I can take stress away

A place where I can remove dark clouds

And bring infinite life to the sun

Get Away

I just want to get away
As it's a new day and I'm not involved
Excommunicating myself should help my problems get solved
As I draw a line to distance me from the fake
To cowards I don't relate and haters I don't appreciate

I'm desperate to get away
From the idiocy of society
With teenage girls getting pregnant and fighting sobriety
Men constantly abusing their women domestically
Teenage boys fighting their parents and acting irresponsibly

I really want to get away
From this cold world and get a sweater
No need for welfare or medicare because life would be better
The stop the violence movement reenacted so no more murdering
World hunger comes to an end so no more pain and suffering

I wish I could get away
To start life over and create a new identity
No one will recognize me except the angel in my dreams
Be granted another chance to create a higher self-esteem
And no longer allow pain to be placed in front of me

Resilient Side

Being Black I

Being black isn't what I'm trying to be
It's what I am!

Because I'm not obnoxious, I'm not black?
Does having aspirations mean I'm not black?
Does wearing my pants around my waist
rather than below my butt mean I'm not black?
Does my desire to make an honest living
instead of selling drugs mean I'm not black?

Being black isn't what I'm trying to be
It's what I am!

Where is there a written rule
That says we have to fit a certain mold
Regardless of what you've seen or been told
You're a stereotypical asshole
Because you're not secure with who you are
You want to try to tell me what I am not
As the plot thickens this needs to stop
Because I don't have to stop
Acting the way I do
To prove anything to you

Who are you?
Do you even know?
Do you have the slightest clue?

Being black isn't what I'm trying to be
It's what I am!

Being Black II

Being black isn't what I'm trying to be
It's what I am!

Who are you?
Do you even know?
Do you have the slightest clue?

Figure that out rather than pass judgment
On another person
Let your narrow minded thoughts
Become extinct before they
Manifest into evil spirits
And it hurts you to blink

Being black isn't what I'm trying to be
It's what I am!

Does me being black intimidate you?
You must think I have an advantage
Because I am not a product of what you see on TV
I am different and you can't stand it
But you have no choice but to handle it
I'm gaining respect and opportunity
Because I command it
I earn everything you demand
And it's all because

Being black isn't what I'm trying to be
It's what I am!

Senryu Intermission

Embrace yourself
Especially when others
Don't want to
Embrace you

We are all made in a certain image. If we don't appreciate the image in which we were created in, then we take for granted the blessings we've received.

Upstage Me

You taunted me, defamed my character, and belittled me!
With no remorse I felt emotionally raped with no vaseline

It's hard for me to believe you tried to upstage me
When I am ten times the man you will ever be
A forty year old virgin is what reminds me of you
As you're twice my age and living behind a bowling alley too

You're a recovering crack addict who wears dentures to replace the teeth you lost
Who's so desperate for a date you hit on your sixty year old virgin boss

Not to mention I caught you masturbating and you were really elated
You're nothing more than the piss in my toilet that I've ejaculated
You're truly hated by everyone except those who you suck up to
Half of them can't stand you either, but they're two faced losers just like you

Another apple a day suck up who gets paid more than you're worth
With your lips permanently attached to your boss's ass I'm surprised they don't hurt

It's a waste of time talking about you, but it's me you're always disrespecting
You don't have what it takes to compete with me or to even stand in my presence
Do you finally get it? Do you see how your life is pathetic?
While my resume is documented and well respected

Who Are You To Me

Who are you to chastise me
Defame my character
Disband me
Doubt and underhand me
You are bland to me
You address me like a distressed banshee
You were insulting towards me and my family
Towards me you were chauvinistic, cocky, and fancy
Now understand me
I am humble until you demand me
To humble and silence you to prove you are not manly
You're an egotistical delinquent who defies and reprimands me

You bite the hand that feeds you
Well I done fed you for the last time
Your selfishness has deprived you of my friendship ties
You forced me to unwind and realize without me you won't survive
The fake tears that you cry
Runs my patience for you dry
You have a slick mouth, but when confronted you lie inside
While I'm laughing at your expense, I see the fear in your eyes
Make me look bad, how stupid of you to even try
Now you've brought on a battle you're not capable to fight
I'll deflate your ego and put a dim to your spotlight
Making you irrelevant like a pathetic parasite

The Rose From The Concrete

Underestimate me!

It seems that's what you do best

As I suppress the duress from emotional distress

I question why you make excuses to exonerate yourself

But my invigoration is a stress reliever itself

Some say I should be more appreciative of you

It will make me emotionally richer

How is that so when you're a cheap bastard

Who wouldn't dish twenty dollars on your children's graduation pictures

Disrespect me!

You treated me like a red-headed stepchild

Similar to Cinderella

Locked away in your dark, cold cellar

Waiting to be set free

As I would try soaring the skies like an angel

You would constantly cut my wings

Contemplative thoughts came to mind of removing you from my life

An emotionally loathing came into sight as I thought of you every night

Appreciate me!

I'm the rose who sprouted from the concrete

And it was not because of you

So don't try to take credit for what you didn't do

Which was produce a phenom with intelligence too

All credit goes to God and your last ex-wife who divorced you

I once questioned the split; over time I understood why she did it

You brought nothing to the table but broken promises and lies

When in need of necessities, child support from you was denied

Senryu Intermission

I've been quiet
For so long now
I will remain
Quiet no longer

In high school I was tried and tested! In college I was bested! Now I'm doing better than what everybody expected!

Man Behind The Man

For years I got comfortable being the man behind the man
But that only brought me to points I didn't understand
Such as being a member of the outsiders clan
Getting taken advantage of, now I seek poetic revenge

Stupid me for giving you the liberty to walk over me

Taking credit for my work, as I try to speak, you'd talk over me

Your inebriated mindset wouldn't allow you to think like me

So you raped me of my dreams by plagiarizing the words I'd speak

Soon you'll hurt like me when karma rears its ugly head

When the work I did for you is dead, you'll come back to me again

For five years you were the center of my trials and tribulations

Your manipulation caused you to undermine my appreciation

My time was wasted, but in the end I'm triumphant now

While you're complacent, I'm twenty steps ahead of you now

You can try to catch up, but you will stumble to the ground

Your frail mentality will continue to let your body down

The man behind the man stands to show you no love
You all abandoned me when in need of help up
You spineless flunkies don't deserve my respect or trust
So continue to be the failures you must

Man Behind Me

Now I see why you wanted me out of the bright spot
   I got the attention you craved which eventually made you hot
      For years you were a joke and the laughing stock
         So you began to scheme and plot on how to knock me off the top

Spineless, jealous, and greedy you are!

As the conspiracy took place, your integrity was then erased
   You couldn't fill my shoes and were in danger of being replaced
      Desperate acts came into play as I was swiftly pushed out of the way
         The example you set for others to follow is a complete and utter disgrace

Mindless, rebellious, and needy you are!

You brag about working your dead end job so freely
   Chasing rodents in a rat infested bowling alley
      I'm a published author and real estate agent with two college degrees
         It's hilarious to me you think you're doing better than me

Timeless, overzealous, and reeky you are!

The conspiracy looked good in theory, but you've failed to execute
   Not that I took you for being geniuses due to your alcohol abuse
      But had half of you picked up a book maybe you'd be smarter; it's true
         The fact that I did obviously made me smarter than you

Intoxicated and irrelevant boozers you are!

I once was the man behind the man, now the man is behind me
   Gladly I see you only possess a ten word vocabulary
      Half of them are profane words that ignite your deficient personality
         But now I see and it's clear to me I'm superior to you as you're behind me

Fabricated and unintelligent losers you are!

Meal Ticket

Your selfishness drove you to disrupt my future
Because your glory days were short lived and now you're a has been
You had no faith in me and went from being a non supporter
To number one cheerleader on the band wagon

That's why I keep my friends close and enemies closer

             I thought friends will do you wrong, but family will screw you twice over

Leaving me the odd man out so I stand out

                But when the money rolls in they all have their hands out

Stalking me and blowing up my phone like dope fiends
Begging me to benefit from my success with no dreams
Kick them to the curb, I'm sorry but it had to be done
I'm not going to be their meal ticket so that thought is dead and gone

I find it hilarious that those who downed me and let me be forgotten

        Along with those who kicked me when I was down and let me hit rock bottom

Are coming back to me now that the shoe is placed on the other foot

            Asking for forgiveness and claiming they were misunderstood

Two Sides Of Betrayal

Although I've built myself up

Into a Redwood tree

My branches and leaves

Lie on two sides of betrayal

One side is for those who piss down my back

Then try to convince me it's rain

Using my name in vain

As I became the law you were supposed to abide by me

But you fabricated the story in which you cried to me

Screw me once, shame on you

Screw me twice, your sanity is in jeopardy

As I can emotionally obliterate the face once known as you

By totally annihilating the weak fight you brought

By starting a revolution of an intuitive mind

Whose personality isn't blind, but hypnotized

Through the indulgence of his grown thoughts

The other side is for treacherous women whose egos I deflate

I can see every day that their intentions are fake

Which I don't appreciate and the thought of it makes me irate

They're physically fine, but attitudes make them an ugly disgrace

Although their brains are ticking the light bulb isn't going off

How stupid they are to think they can interfere with my goals at all

I over step them because it's my time to shine

So they can hate, but they'll just be wasting their time

Senryu Intermission

I speak the truth
Only liars would find
The truth offensive
Not me

Hidden in the valley in the mist of the shadows is a language called truth. Find it, grab it, adopt it, and speak it!

Elephant In The Room

Life is hard enough without others making it harder
Newly departed from my old ways, I now work smarter
Though I still don't fit in
Like the odd man out I get pushed under
Standing on the outside of every faction like a bummer
Alienated while they laugh loud like thunder
I don't get the jokes being told so I stand under
Feeling like acid rain in the middle of the summer

When I questioned finding the other me you all told me no
I reached out for your support and you left me with no hope
By leaving me in the dark with your responses to the letters I wrote
You willing to walk out of my life was what hurt me the most
No call back as you wrote a note
You don't congratulate me; you throw your success in my face and gloat
From that point on I decided to take a stand and an oath
To speak for those who found it hard to digest the hurtful words you spoke

Honesty and dedication helps get closer to accomplishing goals
Maya Angelou once said "you become wise as you get older"
Cockiness and deceitful behavior doesn't help to become bolder
Don't be too stubborn to adopt faith, hope, and love as your new culture

I'm connecting pieces to my puzzle though I suffer from bad karma
Removing you subjects me to living a life of no drama
As I create and motivate multiple crowds with all honors
Those uneducated read my poetry and catch an emotional trauma

Look at my tenure! Top of the mountain?
I've already been here!
While you were at the bottom
Questioning where I see my life in ten years
As my quest to get back continues, I remember
The negative words you spoke saying I would never get there
However I've been there for you; even invaded your front door
Only to help pick up the pieces of your broken face off the floor

I Sing I

I write to you this poem I sing
Because you didn't believe in me

It was a mystery why you resented me; unbeknownst to me
It was because I live a life you could only dream
Deny all you want, but how else do you explain
You criticizing my ambition and slandering my name
Throwing me under the bus so you could step in front of me
In a scandalous environment full of lies and deceit
What upset me was you had the nerve to brag about your life to me
As if you're setting an example for me to follow festively
I'd follow true; if you weren't living in a trailer behind a bowling alley
With no life to look forward to

I write to you this poem I sing
Because you didn't believe in me

Impressively I learned you weren't too excepting of me
You smiled in my face, but laughed behind my back aggressively
As if you were testing me
Now you've created a monster
Who hypothesizes poetically
On strategies to put his haters under
You inadequate loser who defamed my character
I once despised you for who you wanted me to be
If it's anything like you I'll pass; you're a sixty year old virgin
Who gets sexually aroused by your cats

I write to you this poem I sing
Because you didn't believe in me

I Sing II

I write to you this poem I sing
Because you didn't believe in me

You accused me of failing to exceed your expectations
Translation: I was a victim of your retaliation
You lost faith in me; you thought I wasn't going to shine
According to God's plan I was right on time
As God's plan for me
Is to alienate myself from the bad karma you bring
The bad karma you've seen
As you were struck down
For trying to abolish my dreams
My focus was then converted
To stopping you from blocking me
Knocking me; rocking me to sleep
With your illiteracy
That won't allow me to breathe
It's heinous acts from people like you
Who makes me write this poem I sing
Because of you I became a different person
I never wanted to be
You brought emotions out of me
The good, bad, and the ugly
It was in my best interest to leave
As I was graduating from annoyance to insanity

I write to you this poem I sing
Because you didn't believe in me

I rebuke society
For not allowing me
To breathe easy

We live in a world where many people spend too much time focusing on their inner and outer beauty. How about applying that time to fixing your inner and outer ugly?

Bloodstream

You're in my bloodstream and I need you out!

It's amazing how you question my existence
For society when yours is lazy
You slander me, you berate me, and now you hate me
For being who I am so if I fail you blame me
I spoke the truth when I said you were beneath me
You lied when you said the new me wouldn't bring out the old me
You obviously don't know me, but low key
I'm successful now so your narrow minded thoughts can blow me

You're in my bloodstream and I need you out!

It's amazing how you question my existence
For society when you can be
The man who scammed me, stamped me, and slammed me
For being who I am so when I stand you disband me
You claim I have no ambition as you doubt and underhand me
I don't have to prove myself to you because you can't be
Better than me period! Do you understand me?
Now replenish your reputation as mine is greater substantially

You're in my bloodstream and I need you out!

Good Side

Blind City

What kind of thoughts come to mind
Walking into a city that's blind
In search of memories to unwind
But you've broken away so far that they've become
absent from the mind

You wish you could turn back the hands of time
To recap the moments so divine
The feeling of disappointment runs down your spine
As you feel ashamed they don't appreciate your grind

It's almost as if they should've built you a shrine
A monument headlined "Remember The Time"
To show gratitude and respect while they fall in line
And learn from the most influential man how to shine

Still Invisible

I once resented feeling invisible. Now I feel it isn't the worst thing in the world.
As I converse, you overstep me. Your lack of respect show you expect to test me.
Rest assured I don't have to deal with the pressure of losing my social composure.
As I continue to be peaceful and serene, I so come clean and exercise my divinity.

So then you see easy
You can't disrupt me
You can't corrupt me
I will always fly free
Soaring so invincibly
Donating pure energy
Inspiring all the weak
Not to be shy to speak
Defend yourself freely
Be who you want to be
Express yourself openly
Be confident not cocky
A humble life isn't pricy
It's fun and quite nicely
I perform really quietly
I fulfill dreams politely

I might be small physically, but my heart and passion puts me at large mentally.
It is amusing, after the release of The Other Me, people take me more seriously.
Eventually it becomes pragmatic how I can reach out to an audience extensively.
Even though I'm not, I still feel like I'm invisible to the world; no surprise to me.

The Definition

I'm down to extreme measures; my destiny hasn't risen
Life has me backing up into a defensive position
Poets guard your position against this fierce competition
The only way to survive is from your goodness to repentance

I am the cornerstone laying the foundation for your system
I penetrate through multiple angles working the game like a physician
Turning water into wine; no doubt I'm a magician
As I perform the resurgence of a poet you thought was on suspension

I witnessed you misjudging me so here's my redemption
For instance, my reply I supply will strike with a vengeance
My charismatic speech will put your negative thoughts in detention
With the intention to make the sentence cause internal friction

Allow me to take a pause… No… Okay I'll pick it up again
My whole name is interscholastic whereas yours is just a letterman
I'm James R. Dixon also known as the definition to the irrelevant
It's evident they try to claim me, but I see no relation

In the instant I witness my manuscript fails to release tension
I spin it to ensure the message stays intact in its own dimension
I mention the what is and what could be and its importance
What makes more sense is the fact that I am the definition

Senryu Intermission

I'm for the spirit
Of competition but
Don't antagonize me

When you constantly poke at a tiger while in its habitat, the tiger then isn't responsible for its actions.

The Future

My days of being a slave for others are over

Risking my health for someone else will become the world I used to live in

Change will be brought by my body and mind working in unison

You talk as if I've reached my full potential when I haven't

                    You're a has been who's destiny soon became tragic

              I thought demonic thoughts and disbelief in yourself was back then

            Back when I was younger I stated I was the future and not the present

              But back then I was the future and now I'm the present

I'm educating minds with literature to make them feel convinced

That I'm relentless with my words that come off so persistent

I'm consistent, when feeling Teflon bulletproof, I'm resistant

To haters who knock me in an instant, I put them on restriction

            Known as a time out to the adolescent and the infected

              Hating is contagious and I don't respect it

              Instead, I eject it from my life which is already hectic

           But I'm the future and you don't have to except it, but respect it

Trendsetter

I've tuned out of you to check into me
As I stepped out of the crowd's shadow, I was delighted to see
The difference in me! I then dreamed of what could be
Inevitable changes that would mystify my glory

All I ever wanted to be was a trendsetter who inspires,
People to turn their dreams into reality!

I got exotic dancers off poles and gave them career goals
Got teenage girls to stop having babies and focus on being bold
Preached education to teenage boys so they'd do what they're told
Got a few of them out of the streets to see the fast life gets old

All I ever wanted to be was a trendsetter who inspires,
People to become caring and supporting!

I've traded in my designer shoes to feed babies who are hungry
To support kids whose dinner consist of rice, bread, and honey
Hosted toy drives for kids in the community financially starving
Provided opportunities for them in the form of scholarship money

All I ever wanted to be was a trendsetter who inspires,
People to help the less fortunate!

I applied once wasted time to building homes for the homeless
Instilled hope in the minds of the broke and hopeless
I organized several charity events and for those who don't know this
I dropped The Other Me and Broken Silence to help kids get focused

All I ever wanted to be was a trendsetter who inspires,
People to have dignity and self respect!

I sympathize with the abused and confused
Don't be intimidated by something because others don't approve
Don't mutilate your body due to someone saying it fits you
Be you! Don't try to be someone else because they're not you

All I ever wanted to be was a trendsetter who inspires,
People to find peace and be confident!

I've introduced to the masses the fluidity of stability
How the mourning of one's emotions can obtain it spiritually
Adopt positive energy as your companion and not your enemy
Then you'll see confidence and stability is within your reach

All I ever wanted to be was a trendsetter who inspires,
People to turn their dreams into reality!

Senryu Intermission

Those who make good changes
In other's lives
Should be appreciated

I am at my whit's end with inadequate socialites being celebrated for atrocious behavior. It seems as if they get idolized more than those who take time to make a difference in people's lives.

Misunderstood I

My life has been in a frenzy ever since I've dropped The Other Me
My status has grown from locally to nationally
As I irrevocably discussed the other sides of me
The sides they haven't seen; now they want to get close to me
Hopefully I don't see much change in those who know me
Supposedly, women are nicer to me as I try to take things globally
Those who consistently turned me down now never say no to me
So I believe my new outlook on life provides much hope for me

SO

Now I see those new to me questioning my lifestyle
I traded in the baggy clothes for slacks, cardigans, and argyles
I haven't been here in a while so I can't help but to smile
They assume because I'm successful, I'm rich; I just sit and watch money pile
Think again! It didn't come without having to walk ten miles
I had to file an injunction on situations I felt were vile
Projectile vomit is released when I think of my old lifestyle
So I've revamped my identity to match the new name and profile

SO

They say I walk around living life unlike they would
Stuck up and conceited acting like life is all good
Little do they know I was born and raised in their neighborhood
I'm living out my dreams though I feel I'm misunderstood

Misunderstood II

I got rid of my old friends because they were jealous and intolerant
They claim that I've changed and I floss a Mercedes Benz
Unbeknownst to them, I'm not flashy; that's not where my money is spent
I drive a used Suzuki; I upgraded my tent in twenty eleven
So out of shape they get when I chose not to be around them
It's so bad to the point they now see me as an embarrassment
Common sense says I'm no longer good enough for their acceptance
But the blessings I've received makes me refer to them in past tense

NOW

In my social life I was always the topic of discussion
I was so different people felt as if I were Russian
Or speaking Spanish due to my ego not being in combustion
Similar to what theirs is; truth is I was different and they wasn't
They got caught up in society's diabolical substance
Which where I'm from was failure that led to their concussions
They can't digest the fact I chose a new path that caused their financial eruption
It's disgusting how they came to this conclusion and assumption

NOW

They say I walk around living life unlike they would
Stuck up and conceited acting like life is all good
Little do they know I was born and raised in their neighborhood
I'm living out my dreams though I feel I'm misunderstood

The purpose of
The Other Me
Was to clear up
Some misconceptions

There are a chosen few in every crowd who base their satisfaction on judging others. Reason being is because they are not secure with themselves.

Tree Of Life

A
tree
of life
represents
my sacrifice
of what I gave
up to be successful
The liberty I've taken
describes the admiration
displayed in a poetic nation
Each branch is symbolic to an
emotion that I once experienced
Every leaf is a detailed description
of where each emotion is derived from
The stump is the stabilizer that holds my
emotions together to cause the salvation of
my demonic thoughts and they shall reprieve
This is my tree
of life that will
stand as the life
line of my goals

Life

I want to thank God for giving me life
Creating paper
Giving me this pen to write
All of my aspirations and hopes
Goals and dreams; may he not take them away
But multiply them
As I continue to have faith
Manipulate my mind to share my creative mind state
With the world
In hopes that someone can relate
To the things I say as I use them to steer me
As I write, my words come to life, and I speak so clearly
Poetry is my speech
Read and see how it validates me
It inhales breath in my lungs
Giving me life naturally
Like a song unsung
My domestic relationships have been repaired twice
It makes me infallible
And somehow I got life

Wonderful World

World that is in my hands, by

One accomplished goal after another, and

No one can corrupt or interrupt me, now

Distributing my gifted abilities is how I better myself, yes

Excellence is what I will achieve for eternity, so

Rambunctious when it comes to being successful, even

Fulfilling my dreams in a miraculous way, where I

Use my intellectual skills to compensate, for my

Lack of physical abilities to become a poetic athlete, in a

World where only the strongest survive, I

Orally discussed through The Other Me and Broken Silence, why

Really there is no need to compete with me, as I've

Levitated myself to a platform all on my own, in a

Divided world that I've conquered deliberately, I agree

That I've created a wonderful world for me to live in peace!

Once I've drunk
From the tree of life
I've been reborn
My wounds have been healed

You won't know where you're going unless you know where you've been. Find that definitive moment in your life and use it to discover a new being.

Dear Poetry

Dear Poetry,

My goals have been limited
To a condition subsequent
But the substance I provide
Allows me to bring
Multiple dreams to life
That was once unseen
Now no longer a dream
It's reality to me
That I live, breathe, and cherish
Physically, mentally, and emotionally
Caught up in a rapture
Is what it allows me to be

Dear Poetry,

You've illuminated my path
By healing my emotional convulsions
My confined mindset has passed
Into an intuitive mind that is open
I now find myself more focused
Inspired to facilitate an act of notice
That my poetic sense inspires the hopeless
To focus, to take notice, and to avoid being closed in

Dear Poetry,

Thank you for curing me
You soothe me spiritually and move me mentally
Through my knowledge of you
I now understand me

I'm Back

I'm back to old form
Back to seek a reform
Back to rebuild what was torn
Back to rise after the storm

I'm back to living healthy
Back to the focus of being wealthy
Back to worship the one who helps me
Back to abolish being stealthy

I'm back to living how I want to live
Back to display my prerogative
Back to free the minds of young kids
Back to educate those unbeknownst to what I have to give

I'm back to provide inspiration
Back to inspire those impatiently waiting
Back to place my talents in heavy rotation
Back to rebel against being underestimated

I'm back to deliver another manuscript
Back to turn heads all over again
Back with a new sequence of instructions
Back feeling better than I ever did

I'm Back!

Life Line

All the while I keep having this dream
It's starting to haunt me
To the point that I can't sleep
This vision of a family
Three kids and a wife that loves me
It's deranged that this could be my life
I don't even have a girlfriend
Let alone someone to name my wife
But it's like
Little House On the Prairie
With this extended family
My daughters biological mother woke up one morning
And decided this wasn't the life for her
So there I was a single father
Then at the local dairy
I met the soon to be mother of my motherless daughter
As I began to talk to her
Laying a philanthropic foundation
Her irrevocable voice tone
Wouldn't allow me to leave her fatherless daughter
Then quickly I fought her
On us going our separate ways
As it seems we were meant for each other
To create something special

Reversal Of Fortunes

Oh my how the tides have turned; you've become a dictator
I'm a new man, cleansed soul while you're adopting my old behavior
Its obvious you were impatiently waiting for me to make you famous
By insulting the lifestyle of the young and the dangerous

My life compared to yours is enough to silence your hatred
But according to you I'm selfish so a few spiteful words are basic

I'm a selfish man who's lazy with no goals? Boy you're such a kidder!
I'm successful while you're playing the role of your girlfriend's babysitter

Look at what your life has become, seriously it's sad
You're too immature to overlook the way I was in the past
But that was the past and now I'm past you
I'm on an entirely different level and you wouldn't last dude

I thought you were my biggest supporter; come to find out you're a hater
But I'll still be successful despite your envy and mindless behavior

I find it hilarious that you still play this childish game
Insulting and belittling me in hopes I'd feel emotionally maimed

The fact that I don't bend to your will strikes you as a bother
Now you can bask in the glory of being compared to my dream killing father
I have two college degrees and I'm a two time published author
Your accomplishments pale in comparison to mine so I won't even bother

Bones Poem 3
Written by Sasmiere Burrell

Healing Nature

Creator of a beautiful earth, from whose heart outpoured such glamorous treasures, who nourished the soil with healing nature, I honor You for this spectacle called life which is ceaseless to intrigue me and grant You such reverence.

I honor You for the mystique drawn from the mountains and the misty clouds that may arise around them.

I honor You for the gift of joy when able to explore deep forests.

I honor You for the gentle pounding of waves by wind across an oceanfront that glimmers by sun or moonlight.

I honor You for winged creatures that always seem to flutter and float nearby me.

I honor You for the wonderous, merry feeling annually near the season of Your birth.

I honor You for the invisible gusts of your breath which shake the vines and leaves of trees.

I honor You for water that cascades down riverbanks and over many stones.

I honor You for the pillow puff and fluffy shapes of clouds creating majesty through the air.

I honor Thee for Thy healing nature,

Amen.

To veteran artists,

We must continue to lead by example. Young and new artists are following the path we have paved. They are the layer of furnishings that will cover the ground work that we have laid out. I want to thank you for allowing new artists to be a part of the rebuilding process of the arts. Their craft and skills evolve through our teachings. With the goals that each individual artist has, the world of arts will be taken to new heights. This wouldn't be possible if it weren't for a lot of you being open and providing new artists with opportunities to continue to flourish. Be an example and not a demonstration!

James R. Dixon

To aspiring artists,

Take your place in the rebuilding process by applying everything that you've learned. There is plenty of room at the artistic table to set your plate. At the end of the day we are all artists and must support one another. Don't categorize yourself into any particular field. After all, you may start in one area then expand your craft. Use the negative words of the nonbelievers as motivation to push you forward. Eventually they will take you serious and offer their support. Be an example and not a demonstration!

James R. Dixon

For more information on
"Broken Silence", upcoming projects,
or questions, feel free to contact me at:
poetryinvasion@yahoo.com

I want to give a huge thank you to everyone for taking the time out of your busy schedules to rejoin me by reading my second manuscript. This being my second manuscript, I wanted to elaborate a little more from the message of my first book. With Broken Silence being the extension of The Other Me, I wanted to give more truth. I hope many of you can relate to a few poems in this book. Maybe you have experienced a few situations similar to ones that I've been through and have described in Broken Silence. I want to give a special thank you to those who supported The Other Me (My Moment of Honesty)! As mentioned above, if you have any questions for me I urge you to contact me at the e-mail address provided above!

James R. Dixon

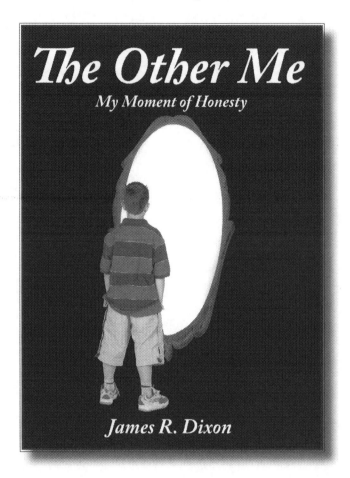

The Other Me was based on what I feel is one of the most important misconceptions about an individual's personality. I'm sure everyone has been perceived in a certain way by others and for the most part those preconceived notions are wrong. With that said, that puts you in the position to have to defend yourself against those who misjudge you. The Other Me poetry book is my self defense. The poems in the book are broken into four sections that determine the makeup of me and my personality. What will make readers gravitate to this book is the fact that it's based on true stories and nothing in this book is fabricated. This is real life with real issues and situations. I like to say the quiet ones have the most to say, but it's getting others to hear them that's the problem. So at the conclusion of this book, maybe a few people will finally hear me.